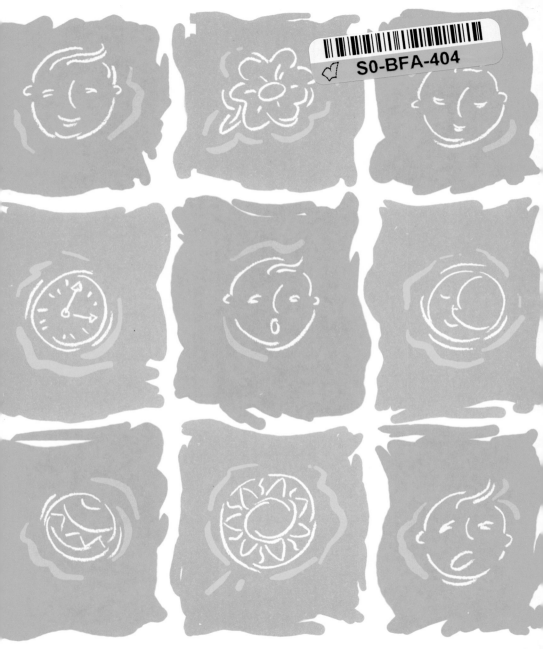

Day-Old Child

First Edition
05 04 03 02 01   5 4 3 2 1

Published by
Gibbs Smith, Publisher
P.O. Box 667
Layton, Utah 84041

Orders: (1-800) 748-5439
www.gibbs-smith.com

Edited by Suzanne Taylor
Designed and produced by Traci O'Very Covey
Printed and bound in China

Library of Congress Cataloging-in-Publication Data

Pearson, Carol Lynn.
Day-old child and other celebrations of motherhood / by Carol Lynn Pearson;
illustrated by Traci O'Very Covey.—1st ed.
p. cm.
ISBN 1-58685-072-5
1. Motherhood—Poetry. 2. Mother and child—Poetry. 3. Infants—Poetry.
4. Mothers—Poetry. I. Title.

PS3566.E227 D39 2001
811'.54—dc21   00-011749

Day-Old Child

And Other Celebrations of Motherhood

by

Carol Lynn Pearson

illustrated by

Traci O'Very Covey

Salt Lake City

My day-old child lay in my arms.
With my lips against his ear
I whispered strongly, "How I wish—
I wish that you could hear.

"I've a hundred wonderful things to say
(A tiny cough and a nod)
Hurry, hurry, hurry, and grow
So I can tell you about God."

My day-old baby's mouth was still
And my words only tickled his ear.
But a kind of a light passed through his eyes
And I saw this thought appear:

"How I wish I had a voice and words;
I've a hundred things to say.
Before I forget I'd tell you of God—
I left Him yesterday."

Needed

The earth needs only nature.
If spring follows snow
If new seeds swell
Earth will go on and on
Content.

I have watched with folded hands
An uneasy guest.

But now suddenly I am nature.
And I am needed
As all tomorrow's orchards
Need the present tree.

How good—
This nine-month indispensability.

The Vow

How could I hide you from hate?
I would, though my arms break with the trying.

Life leans in at the window there
With its bag of dark treasures
Trying for your eyes
So utterly open, so unaware.

You will see men smile over blood
And you will know there is hate.
You may see bombs and butcheries
And you will know there is horror.

Against all this what can I do?
Only vow that before you leave my arms
You will know past ever doubting
That there is love, too.

New Child

I savor
This mutual feast:

You
At my breast
Desperately
Drinking life

And me
Watching
Touching
Sipping eagerly
On your sweet
Evidence
Of immortality.

Mother to Child

Look—
Your little fist fits mine
Like the pit in a plum.

One day and one size
These two hands
Will clasp companionably.

Help me, child.
Forgive me when I fail you.
I'm your mother, true,
But in the end
Merely an older equal
Doing her faltering best
For a dear, small friend.

Impact

If the purple flutter
Of a gossamer wing in Yokohama
Changes the dance of a breeze
On the California coast
(So much a web are we)

What of the stunning vibration
That suddenly sang across the earth
Slightly shifting only everything
For everyone everywhere
The moment I groaned
The blessing of your being
Into birth.

Motherhood has ruined
me for life.

I want to nurse the world
A continent to a breast.

I want to cut up waffles
For all the third world
Send the dictator to his room
Ground the drug dealers
Wash out the pornographers'
Mouths with soap
And spray organized crime
With Black Flag.

I want to make all the politicians
And all the executives sit on
the couch

And memorize the golden rule
And stand up and say it in
unison.

I want to grab a bullhorn
And announce to the world
That the barbecues will stop
Until all the litter—all the
litter—
Has been picked up.

Oh, I could fix everything
If they would all just listen to me.
Listen to me
Listen to me!

I have such illusions of grandeur:
I am a mother.

I did not plant you, true.
But when the season is done—
When the alternate prayers for sun
And for rain are counted—
When the pain of weeding
And the pride of watching
Are through—

Then I will hold you high,
A shining sheaf
Above the thousand seeds grown wild.

Not my planting,
But by heaven my harvest—
My own child.

The little girl unfrowned and then
Sort of smiled when
After hearing the dictionary definition

She was told that what adopted
Really meant was

Searched for
Prayed for
Worked for
Finally gratefully got
Unquestionably on purpose
And loved a lot.

He works at the bank
And has a large desk
And people listen when he talks.

And he takes good care
Of his charges:
Money, certificates
Stocks.

And she stays home
Unnoticed
And every day
Tends treasures
That outshine all the gold
In Fort Knox.

Being a duplex
I have been happy, my dear,
To loan you half the house
Rent-free and furnished
As best I could.

You have been a good
Tenant, all in all
Quiet, yet comfortably there
Tapping friendly on the wall.

But I hear
You have outgrown the place
And are packing up to move.
Well, I will miss
The sweet proximity.
But we will keep in touch.
There are bonds, my dear,

That reach beyond a block
Or a mile or a hemisphere
Born of much love and labor.

I approve the move
And gladly turn from landlady
To neighbor.

I saw a calf born once.
It really was amazing
How soon (all tidied up by
    tongue)
He wobbled off
And the new mother
Went back to grazing.

But you, my little creature
At the top of the animal
    kingdom
You would lie in the pasture
    for months
And wave your fists and cry.

So here we are,
You and I
Tied together in all

The bathings and the dryings
The pickings up and the
    puttings down
And the turnings over
The dressings and the
    undressings
And the powderings and
    the feedings
And the cleanings up of
    the comings out.

I know—
I know what it's all about
This disguised blessing of
    unavoidable touch
Spinning a thousand threads
That encircle us like little lariats.
And before you know it

We're caught.

Calves come for going.
But not—not my little ones.
The Lord thought it all up
This essential intimacy
And he called it good.

He created the heavens and the earth
And the seas, and the naked, needing
Infants crying to be held.
He thought it all up
This clever stratagem.

And yet—
I'll bet he smiled
When he thought about diapering at 4:00 a.m.

Don't Push

The minute the doctor said "push"
I did, and I've got to stop now
Because you're eighteen.

Breathe deeply
Think of something else
Don't push
Don't push.

My garden could not contain
The beauty of you.

I watched you blossom
Then burst into blessings
Seeds winging in the wind
Beyond my field.

Only God can measure the yield
Or knows
All the places where
Your beauty grows.

To My Teenager

What do I do with a child
Who is taller than I?

How quickly you passed
My navel, my shoulder
My chin, my nose.
And now there is
No more of me
To measure you by.
You are off the chart
And it has thrown things
All askew.

How do you look up
To tell a person
What to do?

You can look down
And say

"Hey, the radio
Goes off now."

Height
Means "Now hear this!"
At least pulpits
And stands and stages
Assist in underlining
Amplifying
And being taken seriously.

I have lost my pulpit.
How can I preside?
Future shock is in my eyes
As I look up
And ask if you
Would be willing to
Turn down the radio
Please?

These little boats
Came by currents
I may never know
From oceans I cannot see
Even from my highest hill.

I cherish the cargo
Bless the sea
And thank the eternal itinerary
That harbored them awhile
In me.

Path of a Parent

It starts with
Meditation on the toes of a baby
And leads to spiritual exercise
That would break the best yogi
Sitting cross-legged before his
    lotus:

Serenity—and colic
And three hours sleep last night

Grace—and the puppy feces
On the new carpet

Charity—and screams
In the grocery store when the
Oreos are ripped from white
    knuckles

Harmony—and three
    Halloween costumes

By tomorrow morning:
A clown, a witch
And a washing machine
To go with Stacey's dryer

Honor—and another conference
With the teacher
And possibly the principal

Silence—and the roar of
    motorbike
And rock
And tap shoes on kitchen tile

Acceptance—and all that is dear
Packing up and leaving home

Path to god-consciousness
All begun by
Meditation on the toes of a baby.